YOUR KNOWLEDGE HAS VALUE

Information sharing and psychological support during the COVID-19 pandemic

Vinodhini Yallagandala

Bibliographic information published by the German National Library:

The German National Library lists this publication in the National Bibliography; detailed bibliographic data are available on the Internet at http://dnb.dnb.de.

ISBN: 9783346454362
This book is also available as an ebook.

© GRIN Publishing GmbH
Nymphenburger Straße 86
80636 München

Print and binding: Books on Demand GmbH, Norderstedt, Germany
Printed on acid-free paper from responsible sources.

The present work has been carefully prepared. Nevertheless, authors and publishers do not incur liability for the correctness of information, notes, links and advice as well as any printing errors.

GRIN web shop: https://www.grin.com/document/1036058

ARTICLE ON
INFORMATION SHARING AND PSYCHOLOGICAL SUPPORT DURING COVID

SUBMITTED BY
DR. Y. VINODHINI
PROFESSOR

ANWARULULOOM COLLEGE OF MANAGEMENT
HYDERABAD

SUMMARY OF THE REPORT

NAME OF THE PARTICIPANT	**DR. Y. VINODHINI**
NAME OF THE INSTITUTE	HYDERABAD SCHOOL OF MANAGEMENT
ARTICLE	INFORMATION SHARING AND PROVIDING PSYCHOLOGICAL SUPPORT DURING COVID
NATURE OF THE ACTIVITIES CONDUCTED	GIVING INTERVENTIONS THROUGH INFORMATION SHARING AND SUPPORTING CORONA AFFECTED PATIENTS

Contents

Foreword.. 3

Introduction 4

Review of literature 4

Information sharing 5

Social tagline 6

Psychological interventions 6

Family support 7

Objectives of the Programme... 8

Concern for family members: 10

Experiences shared by COVID patients... 12

Information sharing 13

References 16

Foreword

The study has been taken up as a part of the voluntary work to support the society. The main purpose of this program is to imbibe the qualities of aiming neighbourhood or generation Z to build a society which has a great conscious on empowering society through establishing social entrepreneurship which is beyond commercial aspect of gaining profits through business. It is not mere social responsibility of organizations or nongovernmental organizations but making the next generation to build a society that aims at building greater social tagline with enriched values and enriches lives.

This report has been done with the help of students who has directly involved with the support of the faculty mentors on "Information sharing and providing psychological support during Covid" involved in providing required facilities both physical and psychological support to novel corona virus- Covid patients directly reaching them and collecting feedback on their experiences and taking guidance from the student group and brought about a positive change in their lives.

This has not only helped the students to coordinate and collect the data and involvement but this has aimed at societal development and sustainability which will be enduring and consistent throughout their lives and develops nation building with a social conscious.

Introduction

The coronavirus COVID-19 and the global pandemic has already had a substantial disruptive impact on society, posing major challenges to the provision of mental health services in a time of crisis, and carrying the spectre of an increased burden to mental health, in terms of emerging psychological distress from the pandemic.

Information sharing is a critical element of an effective response to covid-19 outbreaks. The international system of coordination established through the World Health Organization via the International Health Regulations largely relies on governments to communicate timely and accurate information about health risk during an outbreak. This information supports WHO's decision making process for declaring a public health emergency of international concern.

The COVID-19 pandemic information includes the database of COVID-19-patient bio-specimen resources in hospitals, electronic patient health records, ongoing clinical trials and research results on this disease, policies, guidelines, and regulations related to COVID-19, and the COVID-19 outbreak tracking records, and so on.

Working closely with the affected populations and involving them in the response is critical to understanding their needs and finding the most relevant and sustainable solutions.

individuals who will experience the emergence of new mental health distress as a function of being diagnosed with COVID-19, or losing family and loved ones to the illness, or the psychological effects of prolonged social distancing.

Review of literature

Review of literature through secondary sources have been considered for this project on certain parameters namely information sharing, ,hospital management,non-hoppital management siuch as psychosocial support, financial support and family relations The literature has taken as a support for this study to form a basic foundation for engaging in this study empirically to provide a platform for a formal approach.

Information sharing

1. **Goldmann and Galea (2014)** stated in his study that, a standardized, open, collaborative, and virtual data-sharing system is indispensable for timely and adequate distribution of information to relevant parties in research as well as for exchanging and developing clinical expertise and evidence-based solutions.Depression or complicated grief disorder, consistent with the literature on psychological and psychiatric sequel of global emergencies or disasters

2. **Shultz et al. 2015; Shultz and Neria (2013)**. Healthcare system deficits, both in terms of material and human resources (i.e., lack of adequate PPE, infrastructure for digital interventions, staffing) or in mental health professionals not specialized in the psychological approach of crises and emergencies

3. **Duan and Zhu (2020)** specified that the scarcity of human resources led to individual professionals accumulating multiple responsibilities, reducing the effectiveness of their interventions. For this reason, government, policy makers and health managers need to be aware of health systems strengthening for increasing the capacity of mental health professionals, facilitate training for emergency intervention, and monitor workload burdens, especially when sustained over time.

4. **Kumkale et al., 2010; Pornpitakpan, (2004)** mentioned that the source trust as an important indicator of source credibility can affect the persuasive power of messages such that messages from highly trusted sources are more likely to evoke changes in attitudes and behaviors

Social tagline

5. **UN (2020)** stated that although the international COVID-19 pandemic response has been unprecedented in terms of mobilization of resource and finance, there will also be long-term impacts in terms of treatment burden, including mental health, particularly in low resource and conflict settings. Therefore, it is important to evaluate and identify all risk groups and adapt interventions to their specific needs. Among the variables to consider are disease trajectory, severity of clinical symptoms, place of treatment (in-home or out-of-home isolation, ICU, etc.), history of previous trauma and, previous history of mental health problems. Having this information will help classify people at risk and enable specific preventive mental health measures to be put in place.

6. **Bitanihirwe (2016)** studied that societal underestimation of the (short- and long-term) psychological consequences of pandemics and, consequently, limited resources to cope with them

7. **Fan et al. (2015)** analyzed while observing the situation that there is evidence that individuals exposed to public health emergencies have increased psychopathological vulnerability both during and after the potentially traumatic event

Psychological interventions

8. **Zhang et al. (2020).** Mentioned that poor planning and coordination of psychological interventions, especially when they are applied at different levels and by different professionals

9. **Chen Q, Liang M, Li Y, Guo J, Fei D, Wang L, et al.(2020)** mentioned in their study that at the start of the COVID-19 outbreak, the absence of adequate planning of psychological interventions led to fragmented or disorganized implementation, compromising effectiveness and efficacy, and hampering access to available health resources. Any psychological intervention should be planned and coordinated together

6

with all the social-health stakeholders involved, particularly primary healthcare services and specialized mental health services. This maximised the potential for adequate continuity of care even after acute phase of the pandemic recedes.

10. **Loewenstein 2018; Ogden (2019)** observed that there is also a risk attached to early crisis responses, leading to a proliferation of interventions and frameworks associated with an oversupply of well-intentioned but potentially non-evidence based, psychological assistance, often non-governmental organizations (NGO) and the third sector. This is not to say all NGO interventions are compromised, and indeed prevention in mental health is highly desirable. That said, delivery of preventive interventions must be balanced by delivery and/or supervision applied by appropriately qualified professionals

Family support

11. **Olson, (2011)** mentioned that. flexibility in family roles and rules (as opposed to rigidity or chaos) and cohesion (as opposed to disengagement or enmeshment) is most conducive to successfully navigating periods of change

12. **Hawkley & Cacioppo, (2010)** Stated that families are more likely to experience increased social isolation, the inability to access supportive and educational services, and economic difficulties, which may exacerbate stress in many households. In fact, social isolation increases susceptibility to stress and may have harmful effects on both mental and physical health

13. **Greenaway et al., 2014; Reynolds et al., (2008)** observed in their study that parents who are faced with competing demands of limiting social interactions and remaining at home with their children may be particularly vulnerable during this time; research shows that continual close contact under stress is a risk factor for aggressive behaviors and violence

Objectives of the Programme

1. To study the concept of information sharing in the present pandemic
2. To provide both psychosocial support to covid impact patients

I. Objective

To study the concept of information sharing in the present pandemic through student volunteer teams

1. Hospital management teams

a) Sharing the information available

Health professionals, academic institutions, and government agencies are trusted sources of information and that people share information from these sources because they think doing so will increase disease awareness and promote disease prevention. People may also choose to share COVID-19 information from news media, social media, and family as they cope with anxiety, anger, and fear. Taken mutually, a better understanding of the distinct psychological mechanisms underlying health information sharing from different sources can help contribute to more effective sharing of information about COVID-19 prevention and to manage negative emotion contagion during the pandemic.

b) **ICU and** ICU: visited hospitals with the permission of the authorities with personal protection equipment, observed patients enquired with the hospital authorities about the patients checked whether they are provided with sufficient oxygen kits and beds and also looked at the hygiene conditions of the hospital that required to maintain for the patients in-house and admitted in ICU. There has been an acute shortage of oxygen in many hospitals, not much of the hygiene has been maintained by the government hospitals , it was understood that there are many technical lapses in the functioning in the system.

c) **covid vaccine receiver**

Student volunteers visited hospitals to collect information on vaccination and helped the patients how important is to take vaccination, as most of the patients feared of side effects of the vaccine most of the data what vaccine receivers were through social media which has created such panic among them, Student volunteers explained about the importance of vaccination and explained how this vaccination can help in developing antibodies among the vaccinated persons and help fight this corona virus.

Most of the public were not willing to take vaccination due to negative information spread by false media and other members, but they were counseled by the student volunteers and requested them to get vaccinated so as to protect themselves and the society in stopping the spread of corona virus.

d) Precautions required to be taken during pandemic

In spite of taking vaccination they have follow SMS continuous sanitization mask in fact double mask when they go out, and social distancing minimum6 feet distance has to be compulsorily maintained. Lot of awareness hs been created by the group through their network in their neighborhood

e) Requested for plasma donation

Some team of student volunteers had been to covid recovery patients and created awareness among them about the plasma donation as they will become life savers to many, advised them that they not only donate but they get a mental satisfaction for help the fellow being in the society. It required a great effort for the student volunteer to counsel them or encourage them to donate plasma to the patients who are on ventilation.

f) Medicines donation

Student volunteers had pooled funds from the people who were philanthropic natured and they also pooled to buy medicines for the patients who cannot afford to buy them and helped them timely

g) Information of vaccination types and usages of vaccines:

Student volunteer team ahs taken initiative and active participation in making people that there are no side effects and helped them to register on cowin.gov.in portal so that they get registered and helped them to register and schedule for taking the vaccination and both the vaccinations(COVISHIELD AND COVAXIN) have no side effects and required to take them immediately.

2. Non Hospital Management Team
Psycho social support

Negative emotions present in the patients consisting of fatigue, discomfort, and helplessness is caused by high-intensity work, fear and anxiety, Second, self-coping styles included psychological and life adjustment, altruistic acts, team support, and rational cognition. Third, we found growth under pressure, which included increased affection and gratefulness, development of professional responsibility, and self-reflection.

Most of the people were suffering from loneliness, anxiety, fear, fatigue, sleep disorders, and other physical and mental health problems

At the initial stages of spread of information on novel corona virus people had negative emotions and in most of the people still continuing reason behind is due to lack of balanced spiritual ,mental, physical and social health. Any one of the situations are not matched there is a neeed for counseling for the present pandemic situation

Concern for family members:

Families have also been affected by the loss of ordered support found in household systems, such as schools, childcare facilities or physical workplaces, leaving families with the responsibility to cover their functions alone. Family violence has increased due to loss of family member created a strain relationship.

Families have been affected in countless other ways. Loved ones at homes or hospitals have been unable to receive people. Families have remained connected through video calls, disrupting couples' attempts to conceive children

The pandemic unfolds, we urge clinicians and researchers to seek nuanced understanding of the ways families have been affected by various forms of loss, interruption of goals and ambiguity in decision-making.

In addition to *what* families have experienced, investigating *how* families have responded to the changes imposed upon them will be important.

Family coping largely depends on a family's perception of a stressful event and their awareness of and access to resources available to meet its demands

While there may be fewer opportunities to directly intervene in the ways the pandemic has affected families, researchers are well positioned to examine the meanings families have created about their experiences, resources they have identified and accessed, and how relational functioning has been affected or contributes to individual and familial outcomes.

To console moral

Extended periods of confinement have contributed to changes in family stability and functioning, most of the people had developed fear and anxiety basically for those people who lost

II objective

To provide both psychosocial support to covid impact patients

1. The families which were in self quarantine were given psychological support through Families have also spent considerably more time together and those who are in self quarantine require to make the family members feel that they are with the quarantined person and they don't need to panic, it is understood from the studies that most of the peopleare effected with fear of unknown and this fear is making them mentally weak and in turn it is effecting their health and such patients are more prone to heart attack or low level of recovery rate. These family members must provide support with love and affection.

2. **To develop positive feeling among the COVID affected community**

   Once physical health issues are addressed, often more emotional concerns emerge. to offer reassurance and information, the restrictions imposed can contribute to uncertainty and anxiety, and disrupt the ability of residents to use their own coping mechanisms Creating a connection with the new arrivals, and building a relationship, The loss of a beloved relative is one of the most difficult experiences any of us will go through. Being unable to be with your loved one at the moment of death, which feels right and that makes this so much harder. With the emotional relationship and being connected with them with care and genuine concern step strengthening them step by step though emotional tag , creating resilient behavior among the covid patients to bounce back with higher level of inner power and gaining quicker ability for physical well being.

List of activities conducted

Students were divided into teams and they have coordinated on different aspects pertaining to support and help covid patients and potential covid patients and people who lost their beloved ones and primary member have been contacted in person and provided with different forms of support and mentioned above in detail with kind and conscious mind and with greater amount of responsibility and willingness.

Experiences shared by COVID patients

Many had shared their grievance while the student volunteers.

Patient expressed : Testing positive during festival proved to be a great shock. Half the medicines were not available in the nearby shops. Even online pharmacies promised to deliver two days later. So, my treatment started almost 32 hours after testing positive. Thanks to the student volunteers who helped me getting the support of doctors.

Patient 2. when my oxygen level dropped accompanied by restlessness I got panicked a lot but luckily at the verge of the moment I received the support from one of the student stating that we are helping the people who are suffering.

Patient 3. Our entire family tested positive on the same day, lost her grand father to COVID, all of us were told to self quarantine and the social stigma at our apartment, we were not even asked for any help no one opened doors to see us and we were feeling ashamed and guilt with no support from the neighbourhood, thanks to the team who has contacted us with the support of my friend and help us with medicines and groceries.

Outcome of the activity

Covid surveillance dash boards has been initiated through the use of social networks such as watsapp, instagram among the known circle and neighbourhood and relatives and friends so that anyone who is in need of oxygen, ppe kits, sanitizers, masks, medicines, food and essentials to the bereaved families of the covid affected patients also can be reached.

Covid patients to be reached with emotional support has been initiated by the group of students those who could not manage this pathetic situation as many families whom approached are financially weak and mentally affected people due to this crisis

Information sharing

Public awareness campaigns about the virus, about the disease and pandemic and about how best to achieve individual protection from viral exposure.

Students advised them that insecure exposure to hospitalized patients, confirmed cases in self-isolation, or suspected carriers must be avoided.

Students specifically informed the covid patients about the severity of the second wave of the situation in India and only self discipline and immunity can help them out to protect from this viral exposure.

Students team reached hospitals and observed the pathetic situation supported through their references about the oxygen kits, beds in hospitals, supported by paying the patients bills through pooling funds and this has been a great outcome in their behavior in supporting patients both financially and psychologically

Non Hospital Maintenance

Covid has inescapably grounded high levels of public suffering, taking supportive actions and maintaining everyday provisions and some basic protection (eg, face masks) are steps that have met some of the known members of them such as(relatives, neighbourhood, friends etc.,) expectations and have potentially prevented panic.

Covid patients have adopted the guidance of students by following SMS(sanitization, Mask and Social distancing) students explained them how to wear masks, frequent sanitization and firm social distance has been followed by people.

Supporting patients to pragmatically access a private space at home and advised them to listen to some light music or pursue an in-house hobby such as playing guitar, learning some online courses by engaging themselves or nurturing their passion following quarantine norms instead of feeling isolated and going to depression. The outcome has been very productive by engaging them into pursuing their passion.

Positive impact on patients

Obtained from recovered COVID-19 patients who had established humoral immunity against the virus, contains a large quantity of neutralizing antibodies capable of neutralizing

Provided emotional support to families:

Emotional contamination is an important tagline and it has to be connected. Psychological well being very signicant in the present pandemic situation, the children who lost the parents, the parents who lost their solechild, the adult parent lost their older parent, many families during this 2nd covid has lost their beloved ones or lost their sole bread earners. Some of the team members offered guidance and coordination on how to manage the pandemic to avoid their confusion and, importantly encouraged them to have a cordial relation as family is a biggest strength both in odds and in joy moments, they supported them financially and morally they also alerted them that in case there is any voilece at family the entire family get distracted and this will not fetch them any thing. Such family support has really impacted the families and they were able to maintain emotional balance. Families have found creative solutions through resilience and coping alongside. Families have likely struggled as a result of these losses.

Provided groceries and clothes:

Student volunteers had distributed groceries for one month by taking the support of some philanthropists, interested people, neighbourhood, to helppeople come out of this situation, We may not support them life long but during this crisis a small help will be a great gratitude for them

Meditation and YOGA:

While interacting with the deceased families, COVID patients, and potential covid patients and neighborhood, relatives, friends and fellow group members have altogether insisted upon all the members of the above mentioned that they must practice YOGA and Meditation especially with covid patients they were given a session by the team members to adopt micro YOGA and meditation while being rested on their beds they can do micro yoga and meditation without much strain to their muscles

Most importantly we made them practice Bhastrika, bhramari and lom vilom for the patients who had problem with breathing and this exercise helped them to cope up with breathing problems along with medicines and diet. There has been a positive change among the COVID patients, not only them but even other people had a great impact on practicing YOGA and Meditation They assured us that they would make it as their lifestyle forever..

Providing Home Made Remedies

Advising the people to consume ginger tea, turmeric to be added in milk, while consuming, mixing of cloves, basil leaves, pepper to consume as a prevention of getting corona virus, cinnamom also can be consumed for immune boosting.

References

1. Al-Rabiaah A, Temsah M-H, Al-Eyadhy AA, Hasan GM, Al-Zamil F, Al-Subaie S, et al. Middle East Respiratory Syndrome-Corona Virus (MERS-CoV) associated stress among medical students at a university teaching hospital in Saudi Arabia. *Journal of Infection and Public Health.* 2020 doi: 10.1016/j.jiph.2020.01.005. [PMC free article] [PubMed] [CrossRef] [Google Scholar]

2. Bitanihirwe BKY. Monitoring and managing mental health in the wake of Ebola. *Annali dell'Istituto Superiore Di Sanita.* 2016;52(3):320–322. doi: 10.4415/ANN_16_03_02. [PubMed] [CrossRef] [Google Scholar]

3. Chen Q, Liang M, Li Y, Guo J, Fei D, Wang L, et al. Mental health care for medical staff in China during the COVID-19 outbreak. *Lancet Psychiatry.* 2020;7(4):e15–e16. doi: 10.1016/S2215-0366(20)30078-X. [PMC free article] [PubMed] [CrossRef] [Google Scholar]

4. Duan L, Zhu G. Psychological interventions for people affected by the COVID-19 epidemic. *Lancet Psychiatry.* 2020;7(4):300–302. doi: 10.1016/S2215-0366(20)30073-0. [PMC free article] [PubMed] [CrossRef] [Google Scholar]

5. Emanuel EJ, Persad G, Upshur R, Thome B, Parker M, Glickman A, et al. Fair allocation of scarce medical resources in the time of COVID-19. *New England Journal of Medicine.* 2020 doi: 10.1056/NEJMsb2005114. [PubMed] [CrossRef] [Google Scholar]

6. Fan F, Long K, Zhou Y, Zheng Y, Liu X. Longitudinal trajectories of post-traumatic stress disorder symptoms among adolescents after the Wenchuan earthquake in China. *Psychological Medicine.* 2015;45(13):2885–2896. doi: 10.1017/S0033291715000884. [PubMed] [CrossRef] [Google Scholar]

7. Gardner PJ, Moallef P. Psychological impact on SARS survivors: Critical review of the English language literature. *Canadian Psychology/Psychologie Canadienne.* 2015;56(1):123–135. doi: 10.1037/a0037973. [CrossRef] [Google Scholar]

8. Goldmann E, Galea S. Mental health consequences of disasters. *Annual Review of Public Health.* 2014;35(1):169–183.   doi: 10.1146/annurev-publhealth-032013-182435. [PubMed] [CrossRef] [Google Scholar]

9. Lee SM, Kang WS, Cho A-R, Kim T, Park JK. Psychological impact of the 2015 MERS outbreak on   hospital   workers   and   quarantined   hemodialysis   patients. *Comprehensive Psychiatry.* 2018;87:123–127.   doi: 10.1016/j.comppsych.2018.10.003. [PMC   free article] [PubMed] [CrossRef] [Google Scholar]

10. Li Q, Guan X, Wu P, Wang X, Zhou L, Tong Y, et al. Early transmission dynamics in Wuhan, China, of novel coronavirus-infected pneumonia. *New England Journal of Medicine.* 2020 doi: 10.1056/NEJMoa2001316. [PMC free article] [PubMed] [CrossRef] [Google Scholar]

11. Loewenstein RJ. Dissociation debates: Everything you know is wrong. *Dialogues in Clinical Neuroscience.* 2018;20(3):229–242. [PMC free article] [PubMed] [Google Scholar]

12. Lowen A. *The language of the body.* London: Macmillan General Reference; 1971.

13. Ogden J. Do no harm: Balancing the costs and benefits of patient outcomes in health psychology research   and   practice. *Journal   of   Health   Psychology.* 2019;24(1):25–37.   doi: 10.1177/1359105316648760. [PubMed] [CrossRef] [Google Scholar]

14. United Nations (UN). (2020). *COVID-19 Global Humanitarian Response Plan.* Retrieved April 2, 2020, from https://www.unescap.org/news/covid-19-global-humanitarian-response-plan.

15. Wang C, Pan R, Wan X, Tan Y, Xu L, Ho CS, et al. Immediate psychological responses and associated factors during the initial stage of the 2019 Coronavirus Disease (COVID-19) epidemic among the general population in China. *International Journal of Environmental Research and Public   Health.* 2020;17(5):1729.   doi: 10.3390/ijerph17051729. [PMC   free   article] [PubMed] [CrossRef] [Google Scholar]

16. World Health Organization (WHO). (2020). *Coronavirus disease (COVID-19) technical guidance: Infection prevention and control/WASH.* Retrieved April 2, 2020, from https://www.who.int/emergencies/diseases/novel-coronavirus-2019/technical-guidance/infection-prevention-and-control.

17. Zhang J, Wu W, Zhao X, Zhang W. Recommended psychological crisis intervention response to the 2019 novel coronavirus pneumonia outbreak in China: A model of West China Hospital. *Precision Clinical Medicine.* 2020 doi: 10.1093/pcmedi/pbaa006. [CrossRef] [Google Scholar]

18. Zhou X. Psychological crisis interventions in Sichuan Province during the 2019 novel coronavirus outbreak. *Psychiatry Research.* 2020;286:112895. doi: 10.1016/j.psychres.2020.112895. [PMC free article] [PubMed] [CrossRef] [Google Scholar]

19. Greenaway, K. H., Jetten, J., Ellemers, N., & van Bunderen, L. (2014). The dark side of Running head: inclusion: Undesired acceptance increases aggression. Group Processing & Intergroup Relations, 18(2), 173-1

20. Hawkley, L. C., & Cacioppo, J. T. (2010). Loneliness matters: A theoretical and empirical review of consequences and mechanisms. Annals of Behavioral Medicine, 40(2), 218- 227.

YOUR KNOWLEDGE HAS VALUE

- We will publish your bachelor's and
  master's thesis, essays and papers

- Your own eBook and book -
  sold worldwide in all relevant shops

- Earn money with each sale

Upload your text at www.GRIN.com
and publish for free